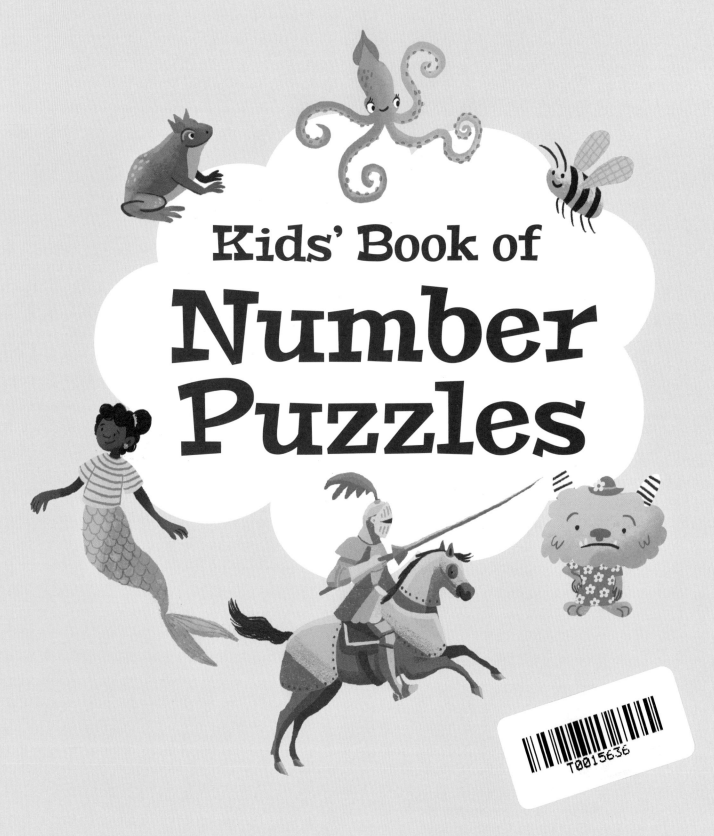

Kids' Book of
Number
Puzzles

T0015636

ARCTURUS

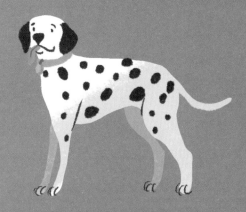

This edition published in 2023 by Arcturus Publishing Limited
26/27 Bickels Yard, 151–153 Bermondsey Street,
London SE1 3HA

Author: Ivy Finnegan
Illustrator: Andrea Castro Naranjo
Designer: Trudi Webb
Editors: Rebecca Razo and Donna Gregory
Design Manager: Jessica Holliland
Editorial Manager: Joe Harris

ISBN: 978-1-3988-2597-0
CH010425NT
Supplier 29, Date 0423, PI 00002509

Printed in China

Number Puzzle Tips

Do you love deciphering patterns, solving word problems, and playing number games? Exercise your brain and have fun at the same time with the awesome activities in this interactive book!

Here are some helpful tips as you go along:

• Read the introduction to each puzzle carefully so you know what to do—sometimes it helps to read it out loud.

• If you get stuck, you can always leave a puzzle and come back to it later.

• When you're ready to check your answers, you'll find them starting on page 87. (No peeking—unless you get really stuck, of course!)

**Ready to get started?
Grab a pencil, turn the page,
and start firing up those
neurons with numbers!**

Polar Count

Are there more polar bears or seals in this Arctic scene? What is the total sum if you add the number of polar bears and the number of seals together?

Tail Talk

Can you solve the number chains on the mermaids' tails? For each, fill in the white space with a mathematical symbol (+, ×, ÷, or −) and then a number between one and five that would make the equation work.

A 60 ___ ×2 − 10 + 15 ÷ 9 = 5

B 7 × 3 − 6 + 10 − 5 ___ = 5

C 12 + 10 ___ − 4 ÷ 8 = 5

The Price of Paddling

This kayaker is looking for a new paddle, but she can't tell which one is the best value. Can you help by working out which paddle is the least expensive? You'll need to work out what the price is after taking off each discount.

30 — $\frac{1}{3}$ off — A

28 — 25% off — B

60 — $\frac{2}{3}$ off — C

72 — 75% off — D

76 — $\frac{3}{4}$ off — E

42 — Half off — F

Monster Family

Minnie the Monster has four children. Each of her children has three children of their own. And each of those children also has four baby monsters of their own. How many monsters are there altogether in Minnie's giant family, including herself?

On the Fairy Farm

Flo the Fairy is selling various items from her farm so she can buy some grufflegoats. Which set of items will earn her the most money? How many grufflegoats will she be able to afford? How many pebbles will she have left over? 100 pebbles equals one gem.

Each bunch of flowers is worth 75 pebbles.

Each piece of ginger is worth one gem.

Each dandelion fluff bale is worth 35 pebbles.

Each grufflegoat costs two gems.

Puddle Puzzle

Fill in the grid so each row, column, and mini-grid has the numbers 1 through 9. Each number can appear only once in a row, column, or mini-grid.

	8	9	6			7		
2		3	1		8	9		
6			3	5	9		1	
			7	6			8	9
		7					5	1
8	6	1			5			4
			4		6	5	9	
3		2	5		7	4		
5	4			9	3		2	

Alligator Snap

The alligators have been playing a game, but they've lost count of their scores. Can you work out who won by completing each calculation? In what order did everyone finish?

Anita
10 + 10 + 11 + 12

Jamal
84 − 44

Pierre
84 ÷ 2

Lily
11 x 4

Easy as Pie

These four pies need to be ready at the same time, but they must be baked for different times.

The first pie takes 40 minutes, the second 30 minutes, the third 15 minutes, and the fourth 10 minutes. Can you help the chef by working out the order the pies should go in the oven from these clues?

Pie D takes twice as long to bake as Pie A.

Pie C will be in the oven longer than Pie B.

Fun with Fungi

Each pair of mushrooms is connected by the same mathematical rule. Can you work out what that rule is and fill in the numbers on the blank mushrooms?

A Whale of a Time

How many seahorses can you spot in this underwater scene? What number do you get if you divide that total by the number of jellyfish? What do you get if you then multiply that number by the number of whales?

Smell the Daisies

The bees pollinate these flowers in order from smallest to largest. Solve the equations to work out the order, and write those numbers in the spaces below.

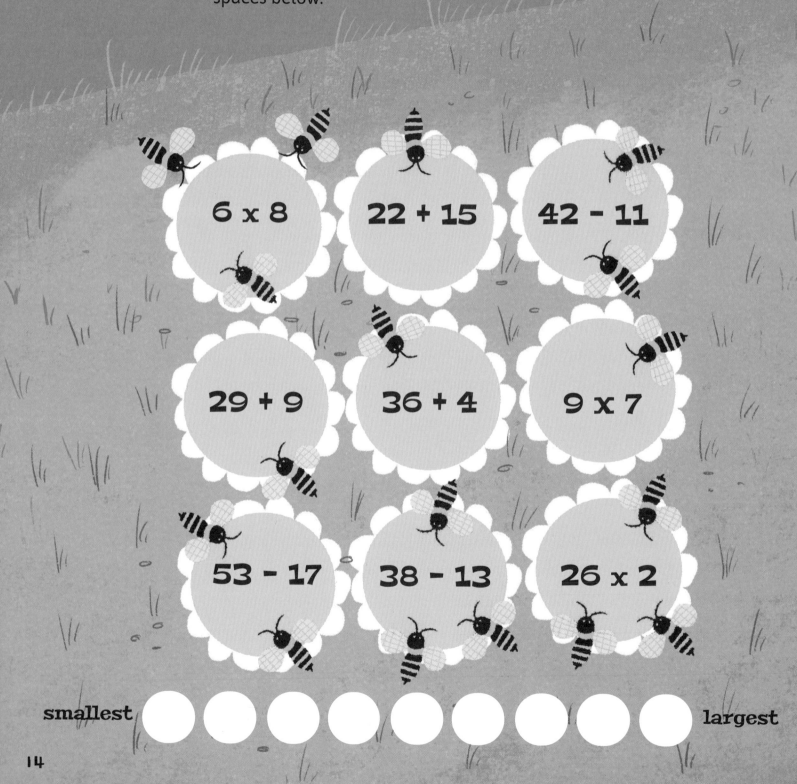

6 x 8

22 + 15

42 – 11

29 + 9

36 + 4

9 x 7

53 – 17

38 – 13

26 x 2

smallest ⬤ ⬤ ⬤ ⬤ ⬤ ⬤ ⬤ ⬤ ⬤ largest

All Stars

Cross out all numbers that are multiples of either six or seven. What number is left?

21 60 49 30

36 12 66

56 28 54 18

14 63 35

24 72 52 48

Lost in the Woods

Can you help the tree planters find their way out of the forest? They can only make their escape by walking along routes that contain multiples of three.

Nutty Numbers

Can you work out what the next number is in this nutty number sequence? Write your answer in the final nut.

4   7   11   18   29

Ant-icipation

Can you solve the four number pyramids on these ant hills? Each square is the result of adding the numbers in the two squares directly beneath it.

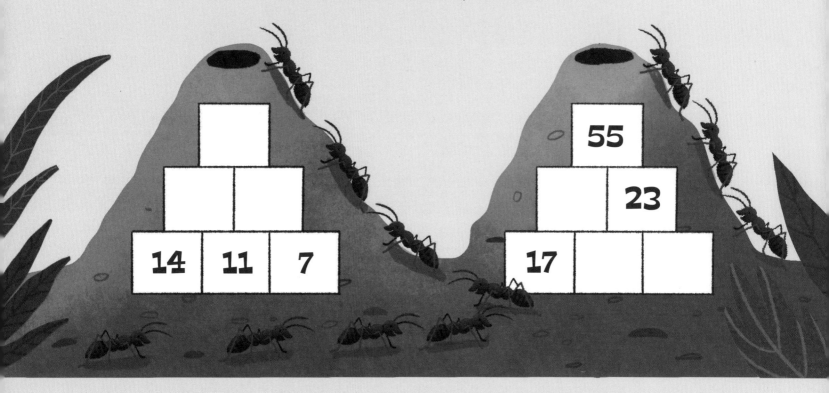

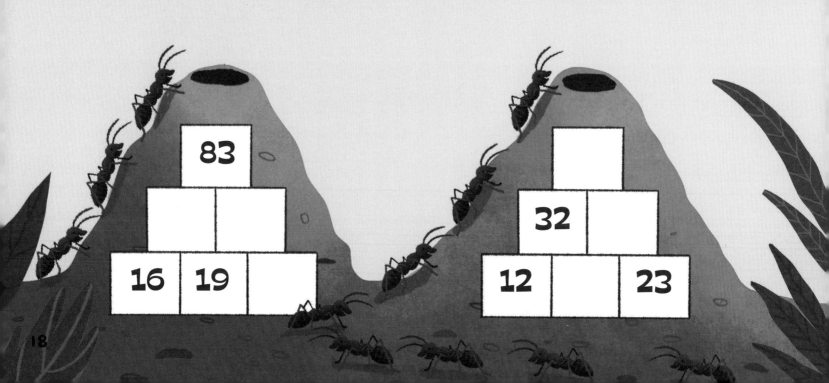

Penguin Puzzle

Can you rearrange the numbers and symbols on the penguins to make a working equation? You must use all of the numbers and symbols one time. Write your answer on the second row of penguins.

The Pirate Code

Pirate Patty is having a party with some of her seafaring friends. Examine the pictures, and then work out the answers to the problems below.

A: Subtract the number of pirates wearing hats from the number of pirates wearing bandanas.

B: Add the number of pirates with red parrots to the number of pirates with green parrots.

C: How many pirates have a pet that isn't a parrot?

D: How many pirates have pets altogether?

E: How many don't have a pet at all?

F: How many pirates combined have swords, eyepatches, and telescopes?

On Your Marks

Keisha is taking part in an athletics competition and is hoping to win the title. There are 15 other competitors. In each round, two competitors must race each other. The loser is knocked out of the competition, and the winner goes on to the next round. How many races must Keisha win to take first prize? How many races will be staged in total during the competition?

Royal Frogs

Each of these royal frog needs its own tiny kingdom. Can you divide the pond up using just three straight lines so there are seven territories with just one frog in each?

Monkey Mathematics

Can you work out the solution to this mathematical dilemma? Start with the first calculation; then apply each of the next calculations in turn before writing your answer in the space at the end.

45   +35   -12   -8   x3   =

Alice in Puzzleland

Help Alice solve this puzzle by adding the missing numbers. Fill in the grid so each row, column, and mini-grid has the numbers 1 through 9. Each number can appear only once in a row, column, or mini-grid.

	1	2	8		5	3		
	8				9		4	
		5	5	4	3		2	1
1	5	6	7			4		
3				1				6
			3	5		8		
		9		4		1		3
8				9			6	4
5	3				1		8	

Racing Ahead

Use the clues to work out the order in which these runners will finish the race.

Claire will finish before Bertie, but after Donald.
Adam will get there after Bertie, but before Ellie.

Kitchen Questions

How many of each of these things can you spot in this busy scene: knives, bananas, bowls, hats, mice? What number do you get when you add all of these items together?

Quit Bugging Me

These four bugs have marked out a race track with grains of rice. Who will come in first? Work out each calculation on the number chain, solving the equations in order from left to right. The bug with the highest total wins first place. Will the winner be the ant, the beetle, the butterfly, or the mayfly?

8 +7 +3 ÷2 x4 +2 =

88 ÷8 +4 x3 -5 +7 =

60 ÷2 -6 x4 +25 ÷11 =

88 -8 ÷4 -9 +5 x2 =

Cruise Control

It's 1 p.m. and these people are leaving on a ferry trip that will take them through different time zones. Use the clues to work out when they will arrive at their final destination.

From Port 1, they will travel eight hours to Port 2, which is three hours ahead of Port 1. They will stay there for two hours.

They will then travel five hours to Port 3, which is two hours behind Port 2. They will stay there for two hours.

They will then travel for three hours to Port 4, which is two hours behind Port 3. They will stay there for two hours.

They will then travel for two hours back to Port 1. What will the local time be when they arrive?

Snail Trail

This snail has already eaten three plants today. One had three leaves, another had four leaves, and the third had five leaves. By the end of the day, it will have eaten the same number of leaves again, plus another third of the total amount. How many leaves will it have eaten altogether?

Spot It

How many total spots are there on all these beetles? If half of them flew away, how many spots would be left?

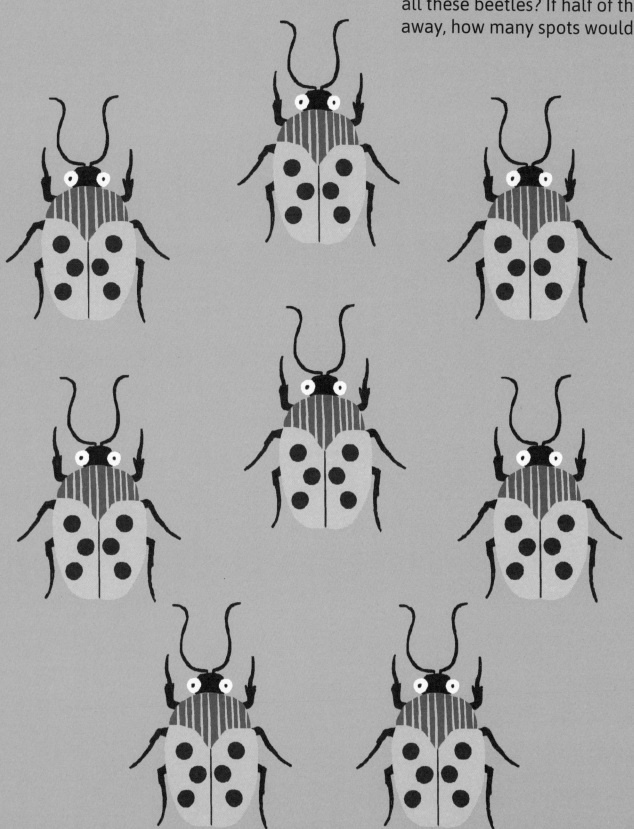

Cookie Cutter

If this cookie machine can make 100 cookies in an hour,
and each cookie has 10 chocolate chips in it, how many
chocolate chips will the machine need every 30 minutes?
How many cookies will it make in a 12-hour shift?

Ball Games

Can you work out which ball's number is a little different to the others?

1   8   27   64

88   125   216

The North Mole

Can you guide this mole through the maze of tunnels to the surface where there are crunchy leaves and flowers to munch on? To make it a bit harder, she must find a route that passes only through numbers in the nine times table.

27   81   32   72   9

12   90

18   11

30

95   72   21   62   13

55

81   83

36   45

51   66

17

39   15

46

63

54   35

108   8

99   67

33

Skipping Stones

Help this scientist cross over the river back to her boat without stepping on any stones that are multiples of nine or four.

5 16 27 4

18

30 28 20 36

29

10 24 81 32

72

57 12

35

21

14

Dragon Money

This dragon needs to pay 100 dragon dollars in rent on the cave she shares with her family. Each red ruby is worth one dragon dollar, each green emerald is worth two dragon dollars, and each blue diamond is worth ten dragon dollars. The gold coins have no value at all! Does she have enough in her basket to pay? If not, how many more of each gem will she need to get from her secret treasure chest?

Dice and Simple

These Vikings are enjoying a game of dice with a difference. The winner is the one with the highest score—on the face-down side of the dice. Can you work out who it is? Remember, the opposite sides of a die always add up to seven.

Pizza Party

José had a super fun pizza party. He ordered four pizzas, each of which had eight slices. Three friends came over to join him and his sister. Each person ate four slices of pizza for dinner. How many slices of pizza are left over? If each guest takes two slices home, how many slices do José and his sister have left?

Busy, Busy Bees

Can you spot the only one of these bees that
has four black stripes on its body?

Through the Window

Can you write numbers into the empty windows so that each calculation is correct?

4 x ◯ = 44

40 ÷ ◯ = 5

440 ÷ ▢ = 44

404 - ▢ = 360

4 x 4 x ▢ = 64

12 ÷ 4 x ▢ = 36

444 - ▢ = 404

44 x ▢ = 176

Purr-amids

Can you solve the four number pyramids on these balls of yarn? Each square is the result of adding the numbers in the two squares directly beneath it.

Pyramid 1:
- Row 3 (top): [ ]
- Row 2: 31, 18
- Row 1 (bottom): [ ], [ ], 5

Pyramid 2:
- Row 3 (top): 77
- Row 2: [ ], 42
- Row 1 (bottom): [ ], [ ], 15

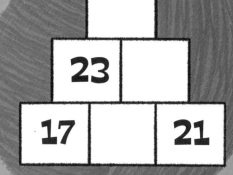

Pyramid 3:
- Row 3 (top): [ ]
- Row 2: 23, [ ]
- Row 1 (bottom): 17, [ ], 21

Pyramid 4:
- Row 3 (top): [ ]
- Row 2: [ ], 36
- Row 1 (bottom): 25, [ ], 20

Clowning Around

Help the clowns solve this puzzle by adding the missing numbers. Fill in the grid so each row, column, and mini-grid has the numbers 1 through 9. Each number can appear only once in a row, column, or mini-grid.

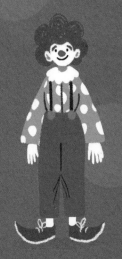

		4	8			3	6	
8		9	3	6	5		4	
					9			
	3		4				5	
9		6			7		1	3
	7		3	6				8
	2	8	9	1		5		4
				7			3	
1			5		4	6	9	

Super Foods

The superhero, Carrotgirl, is doing her weekly shopping. She is buying three carrots, three loaves of bread, one bottle of orange juice, and two cheeses. If she pays with a note worth 500 veggie cents, can you work out how much change she will receive by adding up the cost of all the items she is buying?

35 c each

45 c per loaf

65 c each

55 c per bottle

Coral Celebrations

The fish on the reef have gathered to celebrate Fin the Fish's birthday, but Fin has forgotten how old he is! Can you use the clues to help him work out his age?

It's the number of Andy the Angelfish's stripes times the number of tentacles on Sara the Squid, plus the number of white stripes on Ceri the Clownfish, divided by the number of sea creatures at the party, not including Fin.

Plane and Simple

Study the scene carefully; then answer the following questions:

- What fraction of the planes have propellers?
- What fraction of the planes have just one propeller?
- What fraction of the planes without propellers have their wheels out?
- What fraction of the planes without propellers and with a red tail have a pilot wearing a red hat?

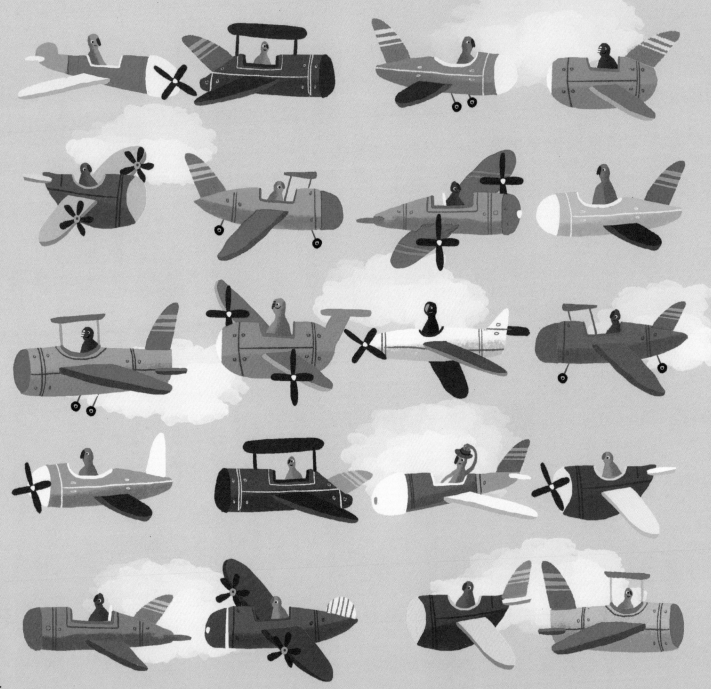

Knead for Speed

These four pizza chefs have been baking all day.
Between them, they have produced 200 pizzas. Use the
clues below to figure out which chef baked the most.

Chef Bob baked five more than $1/4$ of the total.

Chef Billie baked 12 more than 20 percent of the total.

Chef Ben baked $1/8$ plus $1/10$ of the total.

Chef Belle baked the rest.

Well, Well, Well

Can you solve these number chains to work out which gnome will bring their bucket to the top of the well first? Start at the bottom and do each calculation in turn; then write your answer in the space provided at the top. The basket with the highest total will reach the top first.

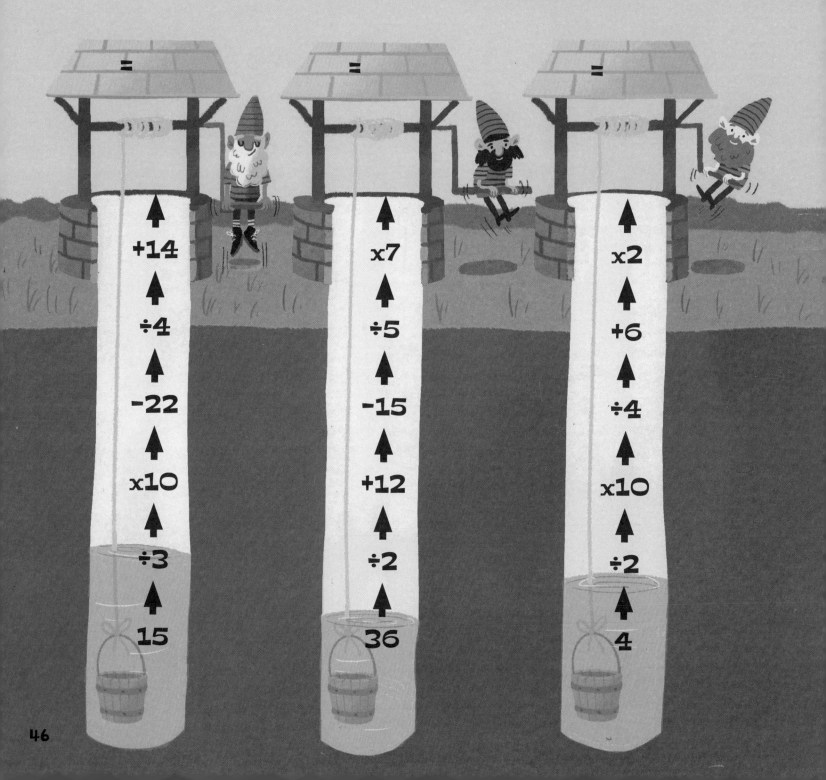

Well 1:
+14
÷4
-22
x10
÷3
15

Well 2:
x7
÷5
-15
+12
÷2
36

Well 3:
x2
+6
÷4
x10
÷2
4

Fairy Nuff

Flora the Fairy is home from visiting her friend Fern. Fern's house is 30 fairy miles away from Flora's and she flew there at a speed of 30 miles per hour. Fern gave Flora some cakes to take home with her, which meant that Flora flew more slowly on the way back at a speed of just 20 miles per hour. What was Flora's average speed for the whole journey there and back?

Mayfly Multiply

Cross out all of the mayflies whose numbers are divisible by either two or three. What number is left?

8 24 30 14

34 2 40 36

12 15 39 6

4 31 3 20

21 40 16 9

Unicorn Carry-On

Can you work out the weight of the unicorns' bags from the calculations on each case? Whose bag is the heaviest? How much do they weigh altogether?

Dolly
9 x 8

Pinkie
10 x 7

Goldie
11 x 6

Magic
15 x 4

Gracie
12 x 5

Having a Blast

This family is enjoying a picnic while watching a fireworks show. How many windows can they see lit up in the skyscrapers? What number do you get if you multiply the number of unlit windows by the number of fireworks in the sky?

Once Upon a Climb

Can you fill in the missing mountain numbers? Each square is the result of multiplying the numbers in the circles connected to it.

This Rocks!

This dig contains many fossil-filled stones. Can you work out the combined number of sides of the stone shapes that are numbered one to ten? Write the total in the space at the bottom.

Total

Toy Store Totals

Aaliyah is shopping for birthday gifts using toy store points. If she spends 295 points, how many wands and balls has she purchased?

45 points each

80 points each

Stick it to 'Em

Remove one stick from the left-hand number of each calculation to make the answers correct.

Shop Till You Drop

These people have been shopping all day. Their bags follow a number sequence from left to right. Can you work out what it is and fill in the missing numbers?

Flower Power

Study these 24 flowers carefully; then answer the following questions:

- What fraction of the total number of flowers have red petals?
- What fraction of the total number of flowers have yellow petals?
- What fraction of the flowers with white petals are being visited by a bee?
- What fraction of the flowers with blue petals have a snail on the stalk?
- What fraction of the total number of snails have an orange shell?

Teacher's Pet

Ms. Bloom has forgotten the four-digit code to open the padlock to her bicycle. Can you use these clues to help her work it out? When you've got it, write the answer on the lock.

The first is the number of points on a triangle plus the number of main points on a compass.

The second is the number of wheels on a bicycle multiplied by the number of wheels on a tricycle.

The third is the number of days in January minus the number of days in February when it's a leap year.

The fourth is the typical number of tentacles on an octopus divided by the number of legs on a bird.

It Bears Representing

How many black and brown bears can you spot in this scene? Some are hiding so you'll need to look carefully. What number do you get if you subtract the number of black bears from the number of brown bears?

Spots and Stripes

How many spots are there on all the giraffes combined? Is the number of giraffe spots greater than or fewer than the number of black stripes on all the zebras combined?

Butterfly Pyramids

Can you solve the four number pyramids for these beautiful butterflies? Each square is the result of adding the numbers in the two squares directly beneath it.

Drink it In

These drinks all follow a sequence. Can you work out
what it is, and fill in the missing numbers?

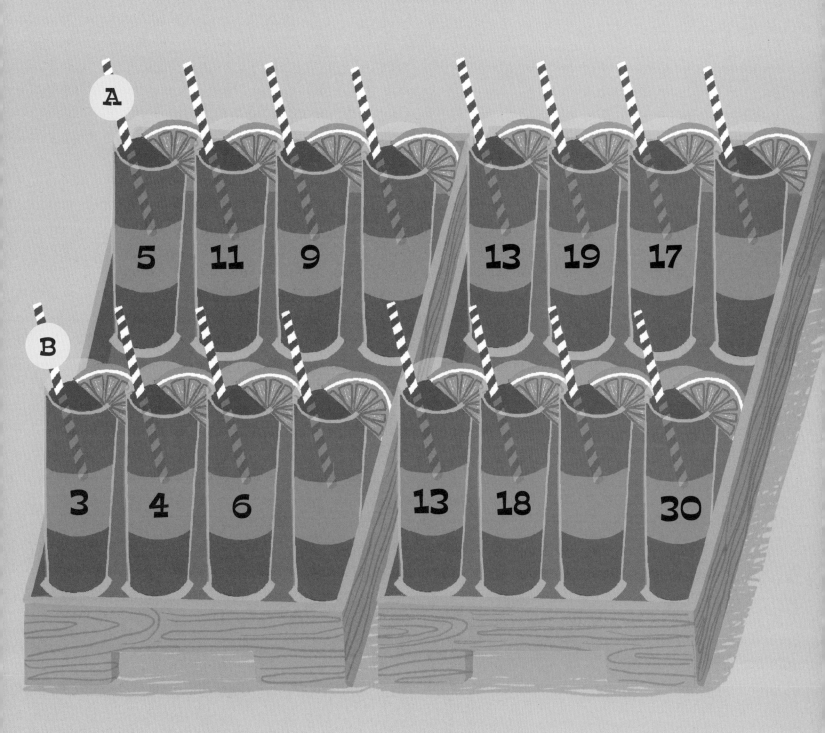

A

5   11   9   13   19   17

B

3   4   6   13   18   30

Lion Around

All these numbers have something in common,
except for one. Can you work out which lion is
the odd one out and why?

Clocking On

This clockmaker wants to set her watch, but she can't remember which of the clocks has the right time. Use the clues to help her work it out.

The current time is between 10 o'clock and noon.

Fifteen minutes ago, the time was not twenty minutes past the hour.

In 15 minutes, it will not be later than 11 o'clock.

Vroom, Vroom, Broomstick

This witch wants to buy a new broomstick. She wants to pick the fastest one, which is the one with the highest number. Solve the number chains, from the bottom to the top, and do each calculation in turn, to help her work out the best broom to buy. Write the answers in the spaces provided.

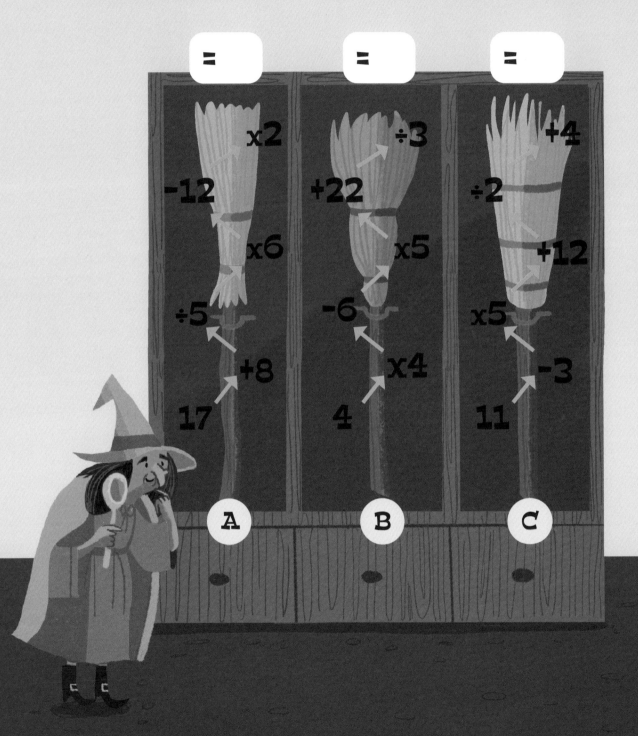

A

x2
−12
x6
÷5
+8
17

B

÷3
+22
x5
−6
x4
4

C

+4
÷2
+12
x5
−3
11

Circus Act

These clowns are trying out for the Big Top competition. Using the clues provided, can you work out whose juggling balls are worth the most? The clown with the highest total is the winner.

Blue = 5 points
Red = 8 points
Green = 10 points

Bobo

Clara

Coco

Cuddles

Locked Out

Grace and her dog, Honey, have been out for a walk, but Grace has forgotten the code to get back into her home. Help her by solving this puzzle. You must place the numbers one through four once each in every row and column. To make it a little harder, you must also obey the "greater than" and the "less than" symbols. The number nearest the point must be smaller than the number on the other side, so 2<3 or 4>1.

Waiter Minute

Two friends are out for lunch at a restaurant in Rome. Saïd orders a salad that costs 11 euros and a lemonade that costs 1.25 euros. Lucy orders a sandwich (7 euros), fries (3 euros), and an apple juice (2.50 euros).

If Lucy pays for both meals, including a 20% tip on the total combined bill, how much will she pay? If the friends split the bill and each pay for their own items, including a 20% tip, how much will they pay individually?

Which Witch

Can you work out which witch is the most powerful? It's the one who is hiding a calculation that equals a multiple of three.

Unlikely Allies

These hawks and rabbits have formed a fast friendship.
How many animals are there altogether? Are there
more hawks or rabbits?

Play it Forward

These friends are trying to cross the bridge in the playground. They will all start on the top step and move to the bottom. Use the clues to work out who will cross in the fewest number of moves.

Charlie

He takes 5 steps forward on his first turn; then 1 step back on his second turn. He repeats this pattern.

Adam

He takes 6 steps forward on his first turn; then 2 steps forward on his second turn. He repeats this pattern.

Beatrice

She takes 7 steps forward on her first turn; then 3 steps back on her second turn. She repeats this pattern.

Daria

She takes 8 steps forward on her first turn; then 4 steps back on her second turn. She repeats this pattern.

Peony for Your Thoughts

This hummingbird is on the lookout for a yummy meal, but which plant tastes the best? Solve the number chains in the leaves to find out. Start at the bottom and apply each calculation in turn. Write your answers in the space at the top. The flower with the highest score is the sweetest.

Chain 1: 6 → ×6 → ÷9 → ×11 → -6 → +17 → =

Chain 2: 50 → -5 → -3 → +5 → ×4 → -88 → =

Chain 3: 21 → ×3 → -31 → -2 → -2 → ×4 → =

Chain 4: 30 → -2 → ×8 → ÷4 → ×2 → -5 → =

How Gem-erous!

King Kamal is very proud of his gem collection. Looking at the treasure chest below and using the clues to help you, can you work out the combined value of all the gems in the chest?

Red: worth 1 coin

Green: worth 4 coins

Blue: worth 8 coins

Yellow: worth 5 coins

Not Kitten Around

Can you help this kitten find the way to her ball of yarn?
To make it more difficult, she can only travel along
routes that contain multiples of seven.

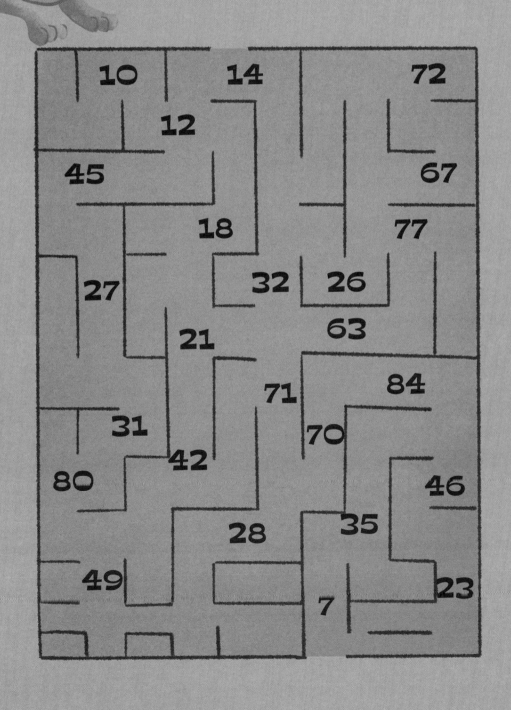

10   14   72

12

45   67

18   77

27   32   26

63

21

71   84

31   70

42

80   46

28   35

49   23

7

Going Coconuts!

Are you a winner at the coconut stand? Starting with the coconut in the bottom right-hand corner, and without taking your pencil off the page, draw six straight lines that pass through all of the coconuts. Your lines can overlap and pass through a coconut more than once.

Going Dotty

Can you work out which of these dotty Dalmatians
has the fewest spots? Circle your answer.

Puppy Pairs

Each person is here to pick up a new puppy from the animal rescue, but there aren't enough puppies for everyone. Match each puppy to its new owner by pairing the equation with its correct answer. Which person doesn't get a puppy to take home?

24   60   22   3   8   6

12 x 5   3 x 2   9 + 15   30 - 8   21 ÷ 7

Turtle Tots

A few weeks ago, this mama turtle laid lots of eggs in different nests on the beach. She laid 10 eggs in one nest, 14 in another, and 19 in a third nest. Not all of the eggs have hatched yet—can you work out how many baby turtles are missing?

Fruit Stall

Can you work out what each of these pieces of fruit costs?

x = 10

x = 24

x = 20

x = 36

Top Tomatoes

Can you work out what the sequence is in each of these sets of tomatoes? Each sequence is written from left to right. Write your answer in the last tomato in each row.

A 56471 64715 47156 71564

B 50 40 31 23

C 2 3 5 7

D 12 24 48 96

Shields Up

Can you solve the number pyramids for these brave knights? Each square is the result of adding the numbers in the two squares directly beneath it.

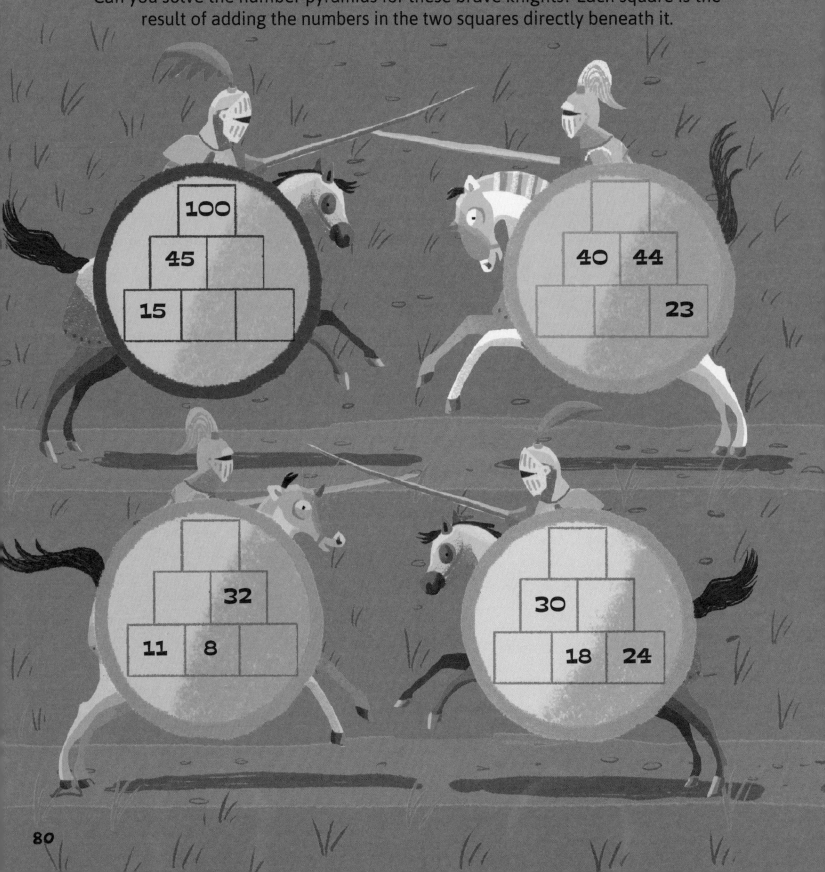

100
45
15

40 44
23

32
11 8

30
18 24

Zoo-doku

Help the zookeeper solve this puzzle by adding the missing numbers. Fill in the grid so each row, column, and mini-grid has the numbers 1 through 9. Each number can appear only once in a row, column, or mini-grid.

3		7		8		4		5
	8				5	6	7	
	6		2				1	9
	5			9			8	
		1			4			
9	3			5		1		6
2		8				9		
		3		2			5	8
1					6			4

A Prickly Problem

Can you match up 10 pairs of identical desert plants? Which plant doesn't have a partner?

The Long Way Home

Can you help Casey find his way home?
To help him, draw a path that follows
only multiples of six.

Hop to It

Cross out all of the insects with a number in the
nine times table. Which one is left over?

Multiplied by Pink

One of these five-a-side soccer teams usually plays in red, and the other team usually plays in white. But their shirts got washed together and now they both play in pink. Can you circle all of the players who usually play in white? They have calculations on their shirts that add up to an odd number.

One Adventurous Cat

Can you help the explorer Kitt-Indiana Bones get inside the mysterious Cat Temple? To get in, you must find the secret door that has an answer to one of the equations below that is a prime number.

$(64 \div 16) + 32 =$

$(27 \times 2) - (9 \times 3) =$

$(100 \div 4) + (4 \times 2) =$

$(22 \times 3) + 17 =$

$(12 \times 5) - (8 \times 2) =$

Answers

4. Polar Count

There are 25 seals and 11 bears for a total of 36.

5. Tail Talk

Mermaid A:
$60 \div 3 \times 2 - 10 + 15 \div 9 = 5$

Mermaid B:
$7 \times 3 - 6 + 10 - 5 \div 4 = 5$

Mermaid C:
$12 + 10 \times 2 - 4 \div 8 = 5$

6. The Price of Paddling

Paddle D is the least expensive.

A: 1/3 off 30 = 20

B: 25% off 28 = 21

C: 2/3 off 60 = 20

D: 75% off 72 = 18

E: ¾ off 76 = 19

F: Half off 42 = 21

7. Monster Family

There are 65 total monsters in Minnie's family.

Minnie (1) + her children (4) + her children's children (4 x 3 = 12) + her children's children's children (12 x 4 = 48).

1 + 4 + 12 + 48 = 65

8. On the Fairy Farm

The flower pile is worth 375 pebbles and will earn Flo the most money (5 x 75 = 375).

The ginger pile is worth 300 pebbles (1 gem = 100 pebbles; 3 x 100 = 300).

The dandelion bale pile is worth 140 pebbles (4 x 35 = 140).

Total number of pebbles: 815 (375 + 300 + 140 = 815).

Flo can afford to buy 4 grufflegoats. She will have 15 pebbles left over.

9. Puddle Puzzle

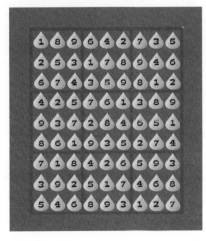

10. Alligator Snap

Lily has 44 points, Anita has 43 points, Pierre has 42 points, and Jamal has 40 points. Lily is the winner, Anita takes second place, Pierre came third, and Jamal finished last.

11. Easy as Pie

The pies should go in the oven in this order:

1st: Pie C for 40 minutes

2nd: Pie D for 30 minutes

3rd: Pie A for 15 minutes

4th: Pie B for 10 minutes

12. Fun with Fungi

Pair 1: 9, 25

Pair 2: 5, 13

Pair 3: 6, 16

Pair 4: 8, 22

Pair 5: 7, 19

The second number of each pair is the first number multiplied by 3, minus 2.

13. A Whale of a Time

There are 12 seahorses and 4 jellyfish.
$12 \div 4 = 3$ and $3 \times 2 = 6$

14. Smell the Daisies

$6 \times 8 = 48$

$22 + 15 = 37$

$42 - 11 = 31$

$29 + 9 = 38$

$36 + 4 = 40$

$9 \times 7 = 63$

$53 - 17 = 36$

$38 - 13 = 25$

$26 \times 2 = 52$

Number boxes at the bottom:
25, 31, 36, 37, 38, 40, 48, 52, 63

15. All Stars

52 is not divisible by either 6 or 7.

16. Lost in the Woods

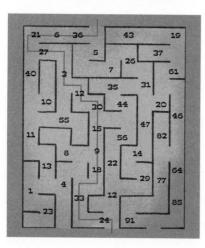

17. Nutty Numbers

The last number is 47. The sequence is that from the third number onward, each number is the sum of the two previous numbers.

18. Ant-icipation

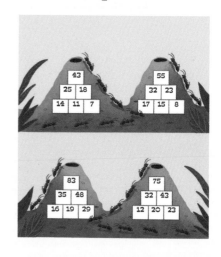

19. Penguin Puzzle

20. The Pirate Code

A: Pirates with bandanas (9) - pirates with hats (7) = 2

B: Pirates with red parrots (5) + pirates with green parrots (4) = 9

C: Lizard (1) + cats (2) + mice (3) = 6

D: Parrots (9) + other pets (5) = 14

E: 11

F: 15

21. On Your Marks

There are 15 races in total. Keisha must win 4 races to take first place.

Round 1:
There are 16 competitors

Round 2:
There are 8 competitors

Round 3:
There are 4 competitors

Round 4:
There are 2 competitors

22. Royal Frogs

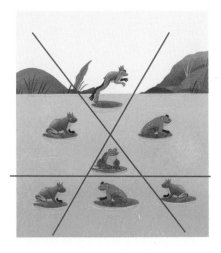

23. Monkey Mathematics

$$45 + 35 = 80$$
$$80 - 12 = 68$$
$$68 - 8 = 60$$
$$60 \times 3 = 180$$

24. Alice in Puzzleland

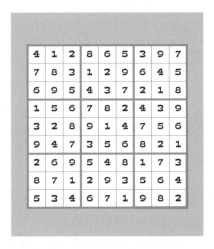

25. Racing Ahead

The runners will finish in the following order: Donald, Claire, Bertie, Adam, Ellie.

26. Kitchen Questions

There are 26 items:
5 knives, 3 bananas, 10 bowls, 4 hats, 4 mice

27. Quit Bugging Me

The mayfly is the winner.

$$8 + 7 + 3 \div 2 \times 4 + 2 = 38$$

$$88 \div 8 + 4 \times 3 - 5 + 7 = 47$$

$$60 \div 2 - 6 \times 4 + 25 \div 11 = 11$$

$$88 - 8 \div 4 - 9 + 5 \times 2 = 32$$

28. Cruise Control

The whole journey will take 24 hours. Because they will end up in the place they began, the local time will be 1 p.m. The information about the time zones isn't needed to help work out the answer.

29. Snail Trail

$3 + 4 + 5 = 12$

$12 \times 2 = 24$

$24 \div 3 = 8$

$24 + 8 = 32$

The snail will have eaten 32 leaves in total.

30. Spot It

There are 8 beetles. Each beetle has 6 spots, so there are 48 spots in total. If half fly away, there will be 4 beetles with a total of 24 spots.

31. Cookie Cutter

The machine will need 500 chocolate chips every 30 minutes ($50 \times 10 = 500$). The machine will make 1,200 cookies in a 12-hour shift.

32. Ball Games

88 is the odd one out, as it's the only number that's not a cube number. A cube number is the result when a number has been multiplied by itself twice.

$1 \times 1 \times 1 = 1$

$2 \times 2 \times 2 = 8$

$3 \times 3 \times 3 = 27$

$4 \times 4 \times 4 = 64$

$5 \times 5 \times 5 = 125$

$6 \times 6 \times 6 = 216$

33. The North Mole

34. Skipping Stones

35. Dragon Money

7 (diamonds) x 10 = 70 dragon dollars

6 (emeralds) x 2 = 12 dragon dollars

5 (rubies) x 1 = 5 dragon dollars

Total = 87 dragon dollars

She will need one more of each type of gem to make the rent this month.

36. Dice and Simple

Norah has scored $3 + 5 = 8$

Noah has scored $5 + 2 = 7$

Nelson has scored $1 + 4 = 5$

Naomi has scored $6 + 1 = 7$

Norah is the winner.

37. Pizza Party

There were 32 slices of pizza. Five people ate 20 slices of pizza in total, so there were 12 slices left over. Three people each took home two slices, so there were 6 slices left over.

38. Busy, Busy Bees

39. Through the Window

4 x 11 = 44

40 ÷ 8 = 5

440 ÷ 10 = 44

404 − 44 = 360

4 x 4 x 4 = 64

12 ÷ 4 x 9 = 36

444 − 40 = 404

44 x 4 = 176

40. Purr-amids

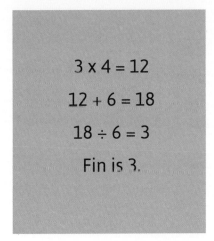

41. Clowning Around

7	5	4	8	2	1	3	6	9
8	1	9	3	6	5	2	4	7
3	6	2	7	4	9	1	8	5
2	3	1	4	9	8	7	5	6
9	8	6	2	5	7	4	1	3
5	4	7	1	3	6	9	2	8
6	2	8	9	1	3	5	7	4
4	9	5	6	7	2	8	3	1
1	7	3	5	8	4	6	9	2

42. Super Foods

She will receive 75c in change.

Carrots: 35c x 3 = 105c

Bread: 45c x 3 = 135c

Orange Juice: 55c x 1 = 55c

Cheese: 65c x 2 = 130c

105 + 135 + 55 + 130 = 425

500 - 425 = 75

43. Coral Celebrations

3 x 4 = 12

12 + 6 = 18

18 ÷ 6 = 3

Fin is 3.

44. Plane and Simple

There are 20 planes in total, of which 8 have propellers, or 2/5.

There are 8 planes with propellers, of which 4 have just 1 propeller, or 1/5.

There are 12 planes without propellers, of which 4 have their wheels out, or 1/3.

There are 6 planes without propellers that have a red tail, of which just one has a pilot wearing a red hat, or 1/6.

45. Knead for Speed

Bob baked 55 pizzas, Billie baked 52 pizzas, Ben baked 45 pizzas, and Belle baked 48 pizzas, so Bob baked the most pizzas.

46. Well, Well, Well

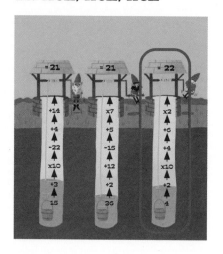

47. Fairy Nuff

Flora's journey was 60 fairy miles in total. She took 1 hour on the way there and 1 hour 30 minutes on the way back.

60 miles ÷ 2.5 hours = 24 miles per hour. So, Flora's average speed was 24 miles per hour.

48. Mayfly Multiply

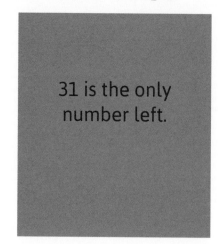

31 is the only number left.

49. Unicorn Carry-On

Dolly: 9 x 8 = 72

Goldie: 11 x 6 = 66

Pinkie: 10 x 7 = 70

Magic: 15 x 4 = 60

Gracie: 12 x 5 = 60

72 + 66 + 70 + 60 + 60 = 328.

Dolly's bag is the heaviest. Together, the unicorns' bags weigh 328.

50. Having a Blast

There are 31 lit windows. If you multiply the 9 unlit windows by the 10 fireworks in the sky, you get 90.

51. Once Upon a Climb

52. This Rocks!

Stones 1, 3, 4, and 10 each have 4 sides for a total of 16.

Stones 2, 8, and 9 each have 8 sides for a total of 24.

Stones 5, 6, and 7 each have 3 sides for a total of 9.

16 + 24 + 9 = 49 total sides.

53. Toy Store Totals

Aaliyah has purchased 3 wands and 2 balls.

54. Stick it to 'Em

55. Shop Till You Drop

From left to right, starting with the first number, the sequence is add three; then subtract two.

The missing numbers are 5 and 9.

56. Flower Power

1/3 of the flowers have red petals.

1/4 of the flowers have yellow petals.

2/5 of the flowers with white petals are being visited by a bee.

1/5 of the flowers with blue petals have a snail on the stalk.

1/2 of the snails have an orange shell.

57. Teacher's Pet

58. It Bears Representing

There are 22 bears in total. If you subtract the 9 black bears from the 13 brown bears, you are left with 4.

59. Spots and Stripes

There are 66 spots on all the giraffes, and there are 75 black stripes on all the zebras. The number of giraffe spots is fewer than the number of zebra stripes.

60. Butterfly Pyramids

61. Drink it In

Sequence A: From left to right, starting with the first number, the sequence is to add six; then subtract two. The missing numbers are 15 and 23.

Sequence B: From left to right, starting with the first number, the sequence is to add one more digit, increasing by one additional digit incrementally as you go (plus 1, plus 2, plus 3, and so on). The missing numbers are 9 and 24.

62. Lion Around

All the numbers are square numbers, except for 7.

63. Clocking On

The correct time is 10:05 a.m.

64. Vroom, Vroom, Broomstick

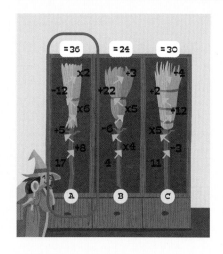

65. Circus Act

Bobo is juggling 3 blue, 1 red, and 2 green for 43 points.

Clara is juggling 2 blue and 3 green for 40 points.

Coco is juggling 1 blue, 3 red, and 1 green for 39 points.

Cuddles is juggling 4 blue, 1 red, and 1 green for 38 points.

Bobo will be the winner.

66. Locked Out

67. Waiter Minute

Combined bill:
11 + 1.25 + 7 + 3 + 2.50 = 24.75 euros
20% of 24.75 = 4.95 tip
Total combined bill: 29.70 euros

Separate bills:
Saïd = 11 + 1.25 = 12.25 euros
20% of 12.25 = 2.45 tip
Saïd's total bill: 14.70 euros

Lucy = 7 + 3 + 2.50 = 12.50 euros
20% of 12.50 = 2.50 tip
Lucy's total bill: 15 euros

68. Which Witch

The witch in blue is the most powerful.
(60 ÷ 4 = 15)

Witch in purple:
8 + 4 + 4 = 16

Witch in orange:
16 x 4 = 64

Witch in black:
1 + 2 + 3 + 4 = 10

Witch in gold:
64 ÷ 8 = 8

69. Unlikely Allies

There are more rabbits (11) than hawks (9).

70. Play it Forward

Adam takes five moves.
Charlie take nine moves.
Beatrice and Daria each take seven moves.

Adam takes the fewest number of moves.

71. Peony for Your Thoughts

72. How Gem-erous!

4 red gems are worth 4 coins
(4 x 1 = 4)

4 green gems are worth 16 coins
(4 x 4 = 16)

4 blue gems are worth 32 coins
(4 x 8 = 32)

5 yellow gems are worth 25 coins
(5 x 5 = 25)

4 + 16 + 32 + 25 = 77

The combined value of the gems in the chest is 77 coins.

73. Not Kitten Around

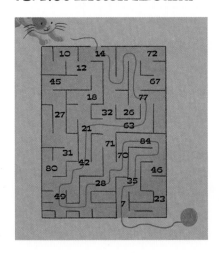

74. Going Coconuts!

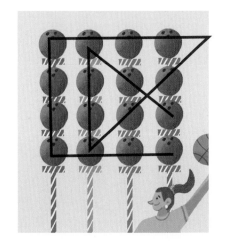

75. Going Dotty

76. Puppy Pairs

The person wearing number 8 didn't get to take a puppy home.

77. Turtle Tots

The total number of eggs laid is 43; there are 39 hatchlings on the beach, so there are 4 baby turtles missing.

78. Fruit Stall

orange (5) x apple (2)

= 10

banana (4) x strawberry (6)

= 24

orange (5) x banana (4) = 20

strawberry (6) x strawberry (6)

= 36

79. Top Tomatoes

Row A: The first digit moves to the end of the number at each step (5 moves after 1; 6 moves after 5, and so on). The missing answer is 15647.

Row B: The number being taken off is reduced by one each step (the first reduction is 10; then 9, 8, and so on). The missing answer is 16.

Row C: These are all prime numbers in ascending order, so the next missing answer is 11.

Row D: These numbers double each time, so the missing answer is 192.

80. Shields Up

81. Zoo-doku

3	1	7	6	8	9	4	2	5
8	2	9	4	1	5	6	7	3
5	6	4	2	3	7	8	1	9
4	5	6	1	9	2	3	8	7
7	8	1	3	6	4	5	9	2
9	3	2	7	5	8	1	4	6
2	7	8	5	4	3	9	6	1
6	4	3	9	2	1	7	5	8
1	9	5	8	7	6	2	3	4

82. A Prickly Problem

83. The Long Way Home

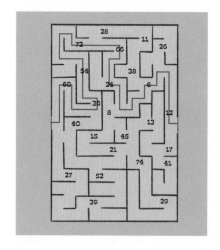

84. Hop to It

85. Multiplied by Pink

86. One Adventurous Cat

(22 x 3) + 17 = 83—a prime number.
(100 ÷ 4) + (4 x 2) = 33
(64 ÷ 16) + 32 = 36
(27 x 2) - (9 x 3) = 27
(12 x 5) - (8 x 2) = 44

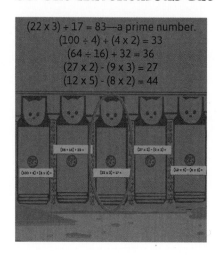